mel bay presents
the bongo book
by trevor salloum

acknowledgments

I would like to thank all the people who helped me compile the information to write this book:

In particular the great *bongoseros:* Armando Peraza, Candido Camero, Jack Costanzo and José Mangual for permitting me to interview them and share their stories and vast experiences with others.

Martin Cohen (President of LP Music Group) for providing the photo of José Mangual, phone contacts and general information. Gene Okamoto (Pearl Corporation) for the photo of Armando Peraza and other contacts. Charlie Rooney for information on Jack Costanzo. David Grierson (CBC Radio) for general information.

John Santos provided insight into the *son* music style. Tomás E. Cruz (Havana, Cuba) for teaching me the subtleties and beauty of the bongos.

Those who assisted in preparing the manuscript: Mary Bellingham for typing, Ann Raghavan and Melanie Bachmann for proofreading, Bob Duplessis who helped in editing and Billy Miller for working through the drum patterns.

My close friend, musician and naturopathic physician Nathan Ehrlich who is a source of inspiration.

Drumming buddy Lonnie Burma for constant feedback and support.

Stan Rule for his friendship and legal advice.

Robin Jarman for providing his musical writing experience and support throughout the project.

My deepest gratitude to Nancy Wise who shared her wealth of knowledge as a publisher in the various stages of the book's development.

My brother Jayce Salloum (New York) and sister Kelly Salloum (Los Angeles) who located some of the musicians for interviews.

And above all, to my parents who instilled in their children the immense value of music.

preface

The Bongo Book is a guide to the art of bongo drumming, demonstrating the wide range of application that the bongos allow.

Currently no listing appears in *Books in Print* devoted solely to bongos. Moreover, few percussion books discuss bongos and those that do devote, at best, only a few pages. Consequently, after discovering this lack of information on the bongos, I became inspired to write this text. It is also disconcerting that the great bongo players *(bongoseros)* of the world have not been given the recognition they deserve. Indeed the *bongoseros* have played a pivotal role in many musical situations, yet are often misnamed, unspecified, or simply ignored.

My interest in both writing a book and playing Afro-Cuban music stems not only from the sparse historical information, but also my musical education. In Toronto I studied percussion with Jim Blackley, Memo Acevedo, Bob Becker, and at York University. After playing jazz for several years I became interested in the *doumbec* (middle-eastern drum) and Latin percussion.

Eventually I became disenchanted with the life-style of a professional musician and decided to return to college to study naturopathic medicine. While attending medical school in Portland, Oregon, I organized jam sessions with other players of Latin music. Once in practice in Canada I felt a lack of musical outlets. Thus, I formed a *rumba* ensemble, teaching others the various components of the music.

To further my education I made several trips to Cuba to study with some of Cuba's finest musicians, including members of Irakere, Roberto Vizcaino (Gonzaldo Rubalcaba), and subsequently Los Munequitos. In addition to teaching privately, I have conducted workshops on Afro-Cuban percussion for schools and colleges in Canada and the United States.

Writing *The Bongo Book* became a passion, at times an obsession. The most exciting aspect was the interaction with the great personalities of Jack Costanzo, Armando Peraza, José Mangual, and Candido Camero. These men are not only great drummers, but truly wonderful human beings who offered their valuable time and recollections.

I hope that this guide will assist in developing the creative art of bongo drumming and enhance enjoyment for all who play and listen. Further comments for future editions are invited.

Trevor Salloum
Kelowna, B.C. 1996

contents

history

Bongos, as we know them today, were first used in the Cuban music called the *son* (pronounced sone). The *son* evolved around 1900 from Oriente province in eastern Cuba. This early rural style included vocals, guitars *(tres),* bass *(botija* or *marimbula),* and percussion. Later the *son* migrated to the more urban centers and trumpet or cornet was added. By the 1920's the *son* had become the most popular dance craze in Havana and soon spread to the United States.

The *son* initially featured the bongos as the only drums. Some of the best recordings that exemplify this style are by the groups Sexteto Habanero, Sexteto Boloña and Septeto Nacional. Later the *son montuno, guaracha, bolero, mambo, guajira,* and other styles developed, often adding the conga drum and *timbales* in addition to the bongos.

As the music evolved so did the drums themselves. Initially bongo heads were tacked on to wood shells and tightened by the heat of the sun or over a flame. However, the natural skin heads presented tension problems with the change in humidity so that drummers were constantly needing to tune the drums. During the 1930-40's metal tuning rods were utilized to circumvent the inconvenience of heating the heads. The development of the original bongos to the present day has been preserved with an extensive collection of bongos in the National Museum of Music in Havana, Cuba.

advantages

Bongos are perhaps one of the most underrated instruments in modern music. The portability of bongos is one of their greatest attributes. Their compact size and light weight allows easy transport; they require almost no servicing and they are very durable. Other than replacing heads occasionally, most parts last for years.

Moreover, bongos are adaptable to many styles of music and have been incorporated in Latin, jazz, rock, folk, flamenco, and symphony. The greater pitch of the bongos also allows greater clarity when performing with other percussion instruments, and because of their virtuosity the *bongosero* in Latin music is given considerable license to improvise throughout the music, perhaps more than any other musician in the group.

The use of bongos gained great popularity in the 40's and 50's with the advent of the beat generation: bongos were used as primary accompaniment to singers and poets like Kenneth Rexroth. The tonal qualities of the bongos blend well with the voice, as evident in Johnny Hartman's 1964 recording of "Joey, Joey, Joey" *(The voice that is* - GRP Records).

description

Bongo drums consist of two hollow, wooden (sometimes fiberglass) shells joined with a center piece (bridge). The shells are single headed and about 6 $\frac{1}{2}$" in height. The smaller drum is called the *macho* (male) and the larger the *hembra* (female). The *macho* is about 7" in diameter and the *hembra* about 8 - 9" in diameter. The shells of the wooden bongos are usually made from oak, walnut, cedar, wild cherry or mahogany staves that are glued and clamped together. Some shells are constructed from one piece of wood and produce a deeper texture to the sound. In Cuba these drums are referred to as *enterizo*. The heads of the bongos are usually thinner than conga drums, thus providing a higher pitch and sensitivity. In general, more extensive finger work is utilized on bongos as compared to congas.

Traditionally, heads were made from mule, goat, and cowhide. Now other skins, including kangaroo, are also being used. In addition, used X-ray film is commonly used on the macho head because of its strength and high pitch when tightened. Generally the *macho* head is thinner than the *hembra* and usually tuned to a fourth or fifth above the *hembra,* although tuning is best determined by personal choice and the style of music. For example, in the early *son* music *bongoseros* would often tune the *hembra* very low to produce the moose call or glissando technique (see ORNAMENTATION p. 39). The *macho* is usually tightened very tight to produce a sharp rim shot.

Various companies manufacture excellent bongo drums in both beginner and professional models. Some popular makes include Latin Percussion, Afro, Toca, MOPERC, Gon Bop, JCR, Skin on Skin, and Juniors.

Bongos are traditionally played in a seated position with the drums held between the legs. Usually the *macho* is on the drummer's left and the *hembra* is on the right.[1] Both feet can be placed flat on the floor with the right oriented perpendicular to the left (see photo below). Alternatively, one foot can be slightly raised off the floor at the heel. This position may facilitate raising the *macho* slightly higher than the *hembra*.

Remember: comfort is the key. The body should be positioned with the back kept straight. Wrists are placed close to the thighs. In some musical situations bongos may be placed on a stand to allow faster movement between various percussion settings.

BONGO POSITIONING

Photo by T. Salloum ©1995

When learning, try not to hold your breath since many problems in muscle tension develop from incorrect breathing. Keep arms, shoulders, back, and neck relaxed.

---

[1] This positioning may be reversed when playing the musical style known as changüí.

The clave is a rhythm that forms the foundation to most Afro-Cuban music. It is a point of reference for all instruments throughout the song. The specific clave pattern is constantly played or implied throughout the music; it is usually played on an instrument known as claves: two hard-wood sticks which are held in a specific way to allow maximum resonance.

There are two main forms of clave in Afro-Cuban music. *Son* clave is the oldest and most common. This is played in the majority of Afro-Cuban music styles including *son, cha-cha-chá, mambo, guaracha, guajira*, etc. The other main clave is known as *rumba* clave. Although *son* clave was originally played in *rumba* (prior to 1950), the *rumba* clave is now the preferred clave by the *rumberos* (players of *rumba*).[1]

SON CLAVE

RUMBA CLAVE

The second note of the clave is known as the *bombo*. This note is often accentuated by certain drummers in Afro-Cuban music. In Cuba, clave is usually written as a one-bar phrase; however in North America most musicians write clave as a two-bar phrase:

SON CLAVE (Cuban Style)

RUMBA CLAVE

---

[1] In writing the musical notation please note that I have used an unconventional methodology, but a very concise and logical approach. This method is used by instructors at the Escuela Nacional de Artes, Cuba's premier musical institution. Although usually applied to congas, I have adapted this notation to the bongos.

Since the two-bar notation is more familiar to most North American musicians, this text will conform to the two-bar format.[2]

The melody of the music can begin on the first bar or the second bar of the clave pattern. When the melody starts on the first bar, North American musicians refer to this as forward clave or 3-2. Alternately when the melody begins on the second bar, they refer to this as reverse clave or 2-3. Cuban musicians typically do not use this terminology, but play the melody the way they feel it best fits the clave.

Two other rhythms that are common in Afro-Cuban music include the *cáscara* and the 6/8 bell pattern. The *cáscara* is a rhythm usually played with a stick on a shell of a drum or a piece of bamboo called a *gua gua*. Usually the pattern is played with two hands.

CASCARA

Note that the right hand is actually playing *rumba* clave while the left plays the remaining notes of the *cáscara*. The 6/8 bell pattern is a rhythm that is used in *rumba columbia, bembé,* and other rhythms indigenous to West Africa. It is usually played on a hoe blade or cowbell:

BELL PATTERN

Clave 6/8

Bell

Note the relation of the clave to the 6/8 bell in the above example. The clave represents the accented notes of the bell pattern.

The three patterns: clave, *cáscara,* and 6/8 bell can be utilized in bongo drumming to develop greater polyrhythms. The chapter on exercises will elaborate further on the topic of polyrhythms.

---

[2] For a more complete discussion on clave, see *Salsa Guide Book* by Rebeca Mauleon or *Afro-Cuban Rhythms for Drum Set* by Frank Malabe and Bob Weiner.

A variety of strokes are incorporated in bongo drumming. Although no standard notation exists, I have, as previously explained, utilized notation that is similar to that which is used at the Escuela Nacional de Arte de Cuba.

 1) **Open** - Usually played with the index finger, middle or first three digits simultaneously. Finger strikes the edge of the drum and rebounds off the head. Stroke is executed with the distal[1] $1/3$ to $2/3$ of digit. Strokes placed closer to the edge of rim produce the higher pitch rim shot.

 2) **Muff** - played by striking the head with the first three fingers and trapping the air between fingers and head without rebounding. Stroke is executed with the distal $1/2$ of digits while maintaining hand in the flat position.

 3) **Slap** - Closed: played by striking the edge of the drum with the cupped hand without rebounding (like grabbing the head of the drum). Open: played by striking the head with a cupped hand and allowing the fingers to rebound, but the heel remains in contact with the edge of the drum. Open and closed slaps can be used interchangeably.

 4) **Muted stroke** - played by lightly pressing the left thumb and thenar eminence against the head while striking with the right index finger.

MANOTEO (heel toe movement)

 (i) Thumb Strike (heel) - played by striking simultaneously the left thumb and thenar eminence against the drum head. When playing the martillo, the thumb remains on the head until the next stroke is completed.

 (ii) Finger Strike (toe) - played by sweeping the palm of the left hand across the drum head towards your right leg. This stroke is executed almost parallel to the axis of the bongos by rotating the left wrist.

---

[1] Throughout the text I have chosen to use anatomical names of reference (e.g. distal, proximal, thenar eminence). Although these words may not be familiar to most readers, they are very specific terms which should clarify the correct position being discussed. Please refer to the glossary for further definitions.

rhythms

Perhaps the most important rhythm on the bongos is the *"martillo"* (meaning hammer). The *martillo* functions much like the ride cymbal in jazz drumming or the *tumbao* of the congas. It creates a groove upon which improvisation can be explored. The *martillo* also complements the conga pattern by reinforcing the left hand of the *conguero* (conga drummer). The *martillo* is a rhythm pattern that can be used in many styles of music and is not confined to Latin music. The rhythmical feel of the tune will dictate whether the *martillo* is appropriate. (See HAND POSITIONS p. 12.)

MARTILLO

	1	R finger strike L thumb press	*macho*
	+	L finger strike	*macho*
	2	R finger strike	*macho*
	+	L thumb strike	*macho*
	3	R finger strike L thumb press	*macho*
	+	L finger strike	*macho*
	4	R finger strike	*hembra*
	+	L thumb strike	*macho*

Hand Positions for Martillo

Position No. 1 - Muted stroke   Beat 1

Position No. 2 - Ⓛ Finger Strike   Beat 1+

Position No. 3 - Ⓡfinger strike   Beat 2

Position No. 4 - Ⓛ Thumb Strike   Beat 2+

Position No. 5 - Muted stroke   Beat 3

Position No. 6 - Ⓛ Finger Strike   Beat 3+

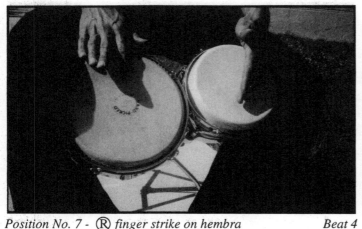

Position No. 7 - Ⓡ finger strike on hembra   Beat 4

Photos by Al Salloum ©1995

Position No. 8 - Ⓛ Thumb Strike   Beat 4

The Manoteo Variation

When playing the *manoteo,* two main styles can be employed. An alternative to the basic pattern (see MANOTEO p. 10) is to emphasize the fingers instead of the wrist. This method accentuates the upbeats of one and three, as in the following example.

Finger strike (toe) variation: manoteo

Instead of rotating the left wrist, flex and extend the fingers with slight extension of the wrist. When executing this movement, the fingers strike the distal side of the head, moving across the head towards the proximal edge of the drum. This stroke finishes a few inches off the proximal edge of the drum. This movement is perpendicular to the axis of the bongos whereas the previous method moves parallel to the axis.

Manoteo:

•**Basic**

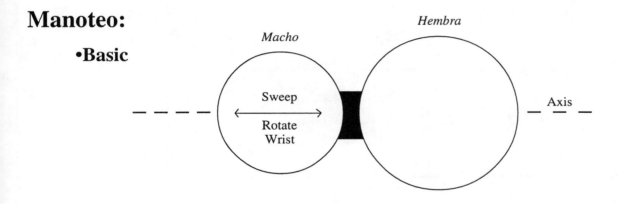

•**Variation**

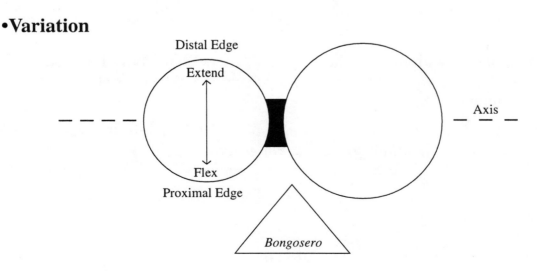

MARTILLO VARIATIONS

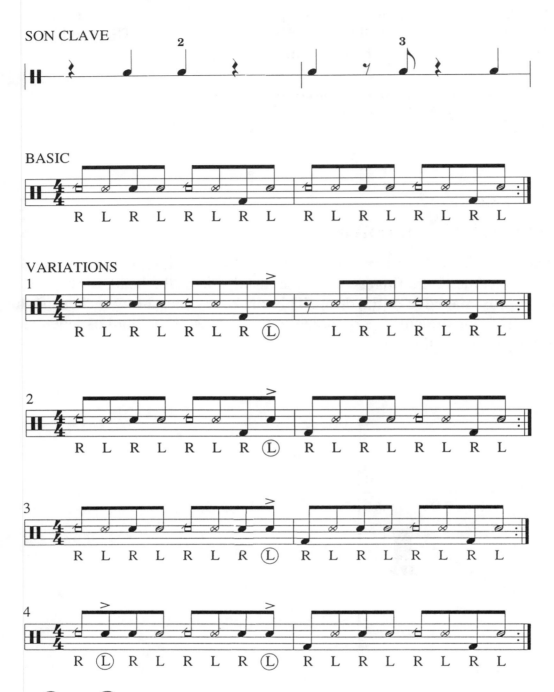

Note: Ⓡ or Ⓛ indicates rim shot

The *martillo* can be played with the rim shot on the 4+ in the 3 or 2 bar of the clave. The *bongosero* will interpret the phrasing of the music and place accents and variations where most appropriate within the context of the music.

When playing the *martillo* a muted stroke is usually preceded by a left thumb strike. When a muted stroke is not preceded by a thumb strike, the *bongosero* can either interpret the muted stroke as a rest or quickly place the left thumb against the *macho* before executing the muted stroke.

MARTILLO VARIATIONS
On Upbeat of Three (3+)

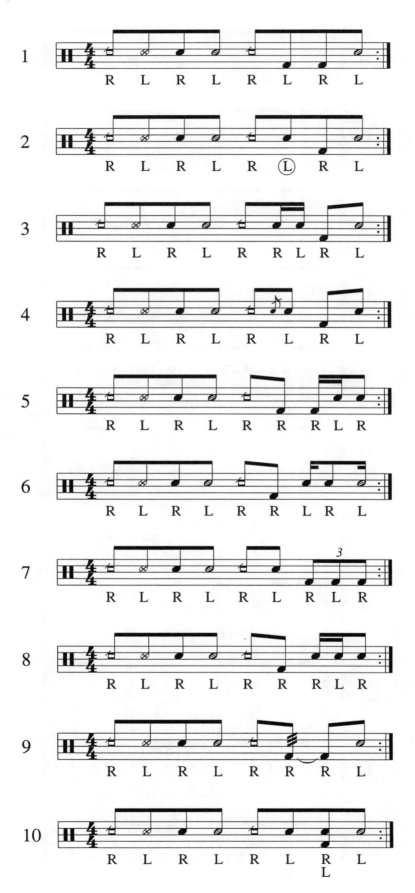

MARTILLO VARIATION
On Downbeat of Three (3)

MARTILLO VARIATIONS
On Downbeat of Three (3)

MARTILLO VARIATIONS
On Downbeat of Three (3)

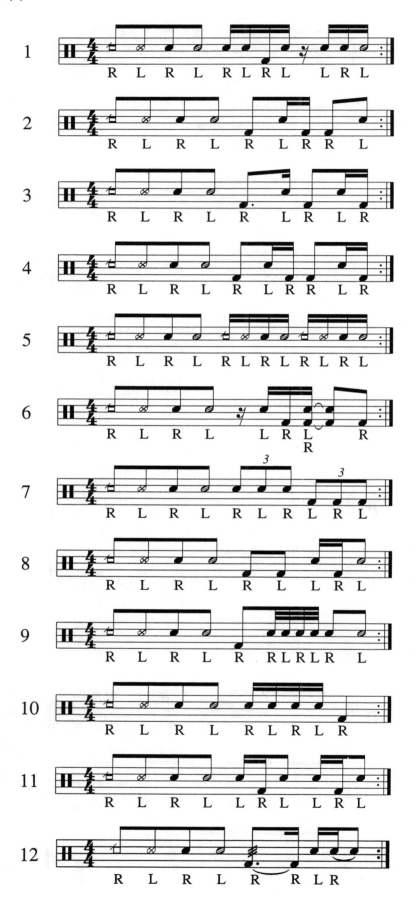

MARTILLO VARIATIONS
On Upbeat of Two (2)

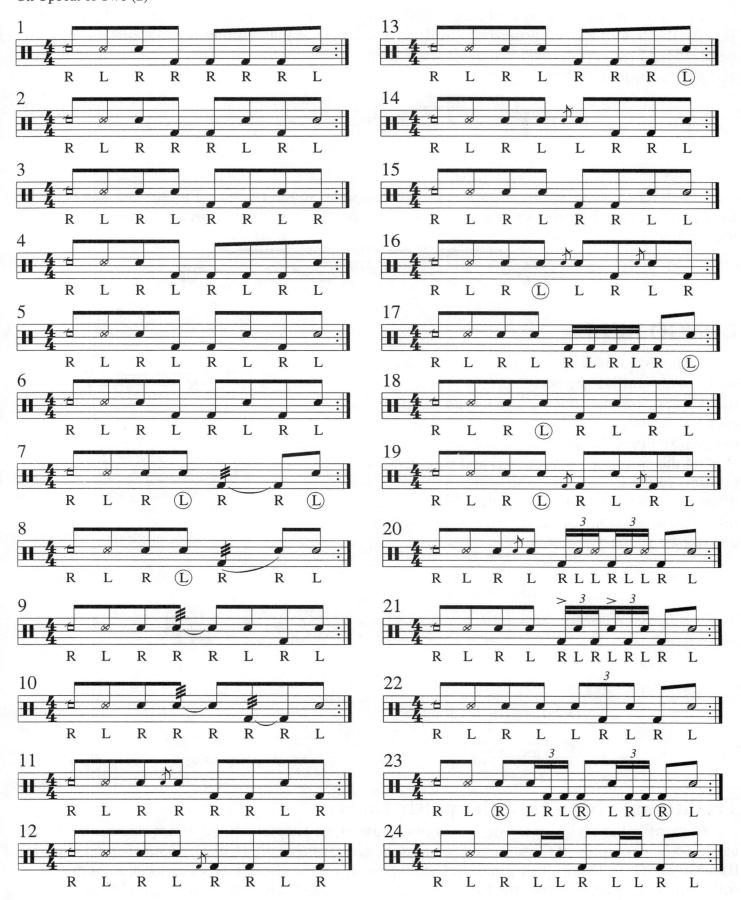

THE BOLERO

Probably the slowest style of Latin music is the *bolero*. It is similar in tempo to ballads in jazz. In the *bolero* the *bongosero* can utilize the *martillo* or play common variations as outlined below. This first variation adds the left-hand fingers utilizing the 5th, 4th, 3rd, and 2nd digits and striking consecutively.

The second variation incorporates a rhythm similar to the *rhumba*. Please note this is not the Cuban *rumba*, but refers to the music/dance craze that was popular in the United States in the 1950's.

BONGO BELL

As noted previously, many musical styles traditionally utilize the bongo drums. These styles include *son, son montuno, guajira, guaracha, mambo, bolero,* and *salsa.* In these styles the *bongosero* plays the *martillo,* variations, and fills. During the *montuno* section (call and response) or sections of greater volume, the *bongosero* will often put down the bongos and play the cowbell (also known as *campana* and *cencerro),* playing one of two primary patterns.

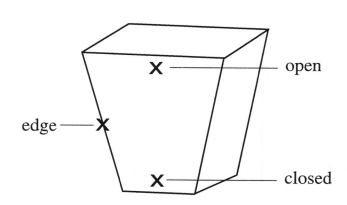

C - closed end or edge of cowbell

O - open

Bongo Bell - Pattern 1

(3-2) Bongo Bell - Pattern 2

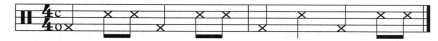

Traditional / Non-Traditional Rhythms

In many other styles of music, the bongos have been adapted although not traditionally used. Some examples of these include *rumba, danzón, songo,* 6/8 (Cuba), *plena, bomba* (Puerto Rico), *merengue* (Dominican Republic), *bossa nova, samba* (Brazil), rock, and jazz. In the following examples the rhythms for the bongos can be used when the *bongosero* is the only percussion instrument or to complement other percussion instruments in the group. These rhythms may also be used as exercises to improve dexterity and provide further ideas for soloing.

JAZZ

When playing jazz rhythms on the bongos the eighth notes although written as even (♪♪) are actually played with a triplet feel (♪ 𝄾 ♪) .

This is similar to drum-set notation in jazz. The following variations can be utilized when playing jazz. Also, try to create your own variations using combinations of these examples.

ROCK

1

2

3

4

BRAZILIAN

Bossa Nova

Samba

AFRO-CUBAN

AFRO

R   L   Ⓡ R L L   Ⓡ

DANZÓN

R R L   L R   L R L R

MOZAMBIQUE

R L R L   R L R   L R L R L R

SONGO

1 

L L R R L R R   L R   L R L R R

2 

R L R R   L   R L R R L L R L

PA CA

The *pa' cá* is a Creole rhythm that has been popularized by Changuito, formerly of Los Van Van, and Angá, of Irakere. Although there are specific bongo patterns to this rhythm, when the conga drum is absent the *bongosero* can play the conga pattern on the bongos.

When playing the conga pattern a stick is held in the left hand and strikes the shell of the drum. Occasionally the drummer will strike the drum head with the stick when improvising on the rhythm. The right hand plays on the drums as indicated.

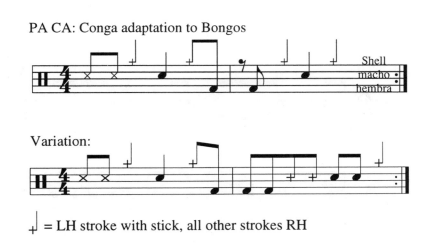

$\downharpoonleft$ = LH stroke with stick, all other strokes RH

PUERTO RICO

Bomba

Plena

DOMINICAN REPUBLIC

Merengue

COLOMBIA

Cumbia

MARTINIQUE

(1) Beguine

(2)

Fills on the bongos can be used at the discretion of the *bongosero*. They should be tasteful, not over played, and always congruent with the clave. Fills can be created from listening to rhythmic phrasing of the other instruments in the band, vocalists, or the rhythm of the melody.

When practicing fills, initially play the fill alone. Then practice playing in four-bar phrases to develop fluidity in moving to and from *martillo* to fills. For example, when playing a one-bar fill, play three bars of *martillo* and one bar of fill. For two-bar fills play two bars of *martillo* and two bars of fill. This transition should occur while maintaining the correct pulse and clave. Once you have mastered the *martillo* with fills, try combining various fills together to create a solo.

In solos the *bongosero* is given considerable liberty to create. Solos are made interesting by starting with simple patterns, then increasing their complexity. Also, melodic pattern and conversation between two drums will enhance the solo. The *bongosero* functions similar to the *quinto* (solo drum) in *rumba,* playing a variety of tones to create color and texture to the music.

One-Bar Fills

27

One-Bar Fills

28

Two-Bar Fills

Fills Derived From Batá Rhythms

1 Inle
   L R L R R L R L

2
   L R L R R L R L

3
   L R R L R R L R R L

4
   L R L L R L L R
          R

5
   R L R L R R L

6
   L L R L R L R L R

Fills Derived From Batá Rhythms

Fills Derived From Batá Rhythms

Oddudua

Shango

Ibbaloque

BONGO SOLO

exercises

Exercises will help warm up muscles of the arms and hands before playing and assist in developing greater speed, strength, and dexterity. Try to spend at least five minutes practicing any of these exercises before playing bongo rhythms or fills. Frequent practice over shorter periods is more beneficial than infrequent practice for longer periods.

The use of a metronome while practicing will help establish steady time. Practice each pattern slowly at first then gradually increase the tempos at higher settings on the metronome. Most of these exercises can be practiced on the *macho,* the *hembra,* or by breaking up the pattern between the two drums.

Single stroke roll

R L R L R L R L R L R L R L R L   R L R L R L R L R L R L R L R L

Double stroke roll

R R L L R R L L R R L L R R L L   R R L L R R L L R R L L R R L L

Triplets

R L R L R L R L R L R L

Flams

R   L   R   L

Paradiddle

R L R R L R L L

Flam combinations:
Triplets

R L R L R L R L R L R L

Sixteenth

R L R L R L R L R L R L R L R L

Paradiddle (flamadiddle)

R L R R L R L L

Sixteen note triplet combinations: Basic

or R L L R L L R L L R L L R L L R L L R L L R L L
    L R R L R R L R R L R R L R R L R R L R R L R R

35

Sixteenth

R L L R L R L L R L R L L R L R L L R L

Gapped triplet

R L L R   L R L L R   L R L L R   L R L L R   L

Eighth note roll

R L L R   R L L R   R L L R   R L L R

Eighth note to sixteenth note triplet with accents:
Son clave

R L R L R L R L   R L R L R L R L

RLRLRLRLRLRLRLRLRLRLRLRLRL   RLRLRLRLRLRLRLRLRLRLRLRLRL

Rumba clave

R L R L R L R L   R L R L R L R L

RLRLRLRLRLRLRLRLRLRLRLRLRL   RLRLRLRLRLRLRLRLRLRLRLRLRL

Cáscara

R L R L R L R L   R L R L R L R L

RLRLRLRLRLRLRLRLRLRL   RLRLRLRLRLRLRLRLRLRL

Manoteo with accents:
Son clave

R L L R L L R L L R L L R L L R L L R L L R L L

R L L R L L R L L R L L R L L R L L R L L R L L

Rumba Clave

R L L R L L R L L R L L R L L R L L R L L R L L

R L L R L L R L L R L L R L L R L L R L L R L L

Cáscara

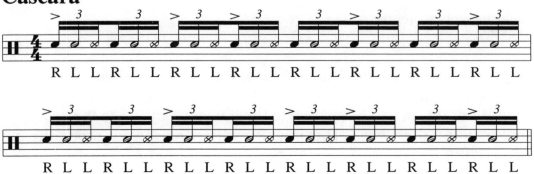

R L L R L L R L L R L L R L L R L L R L L R L L

R L L R L L R L L R L L R L L R L L R L L R L L

37

POLYRHYTHMS

Practice playing one hand (A) on the *macho* with the other hand (B) on the *hembra,* then switch.

	A	B
1	*son* clave	pulse*
2	*rumba* clave	pulse
3	*cáscara*	pulse
4	*cáscara*	*son* clave
5	*cáscara*	*rumba* clave
6	6/8 bell	pulse (2)
7	6/8 bell	quarter (4)
8	6/8 bell	eighth (8)
9	*manoteo* (quarter)	*cáscara*
10	*manoteo* (eighth)	*cáscara*
11	*manoteo* (sixteenth)	*cáscara*
12	*manoteo* (quarter note triplets)	*cáscara*

* As an alternate exercise try replacing upbeats for the pulse.

For further exercises see *Stick Control for the Snare Drummer* by George Lawrence Stone. This text can be easily applied to the bongos to build coordination, endurance, and strength. As well, many other texts written for drum set can be applied to the bongos. Substitute the bass drum line for the *hembra* and snare for the *macho.* This practice will increase your repertoire of ideas and facilitate greater creativity.

ornamentation

Several forms of ornamentation, such as the moose call, are used with the bongo drums much like the conga drums. These sounds provide a variety of tones to add color to the music. The "moose call" was developed with the advent of the *son,* although this technique may be traced to other styles of African drumming. The *bongosero* slides a wetted middle finger, supported by the thumb of the same hand, across a slackened *hembra* head. The friction of rubbing against the head produces a sound similar to a moose call, hence its name. Some refer to this technique as the "glissando."

POSITION FOR MOOSE CALL

Photo by Al Salloum © 1995

Another popular sound is achieved by pressing and moving the left thumb and heel of the hand from the distal edge of the drum to the center, while striking the proximal edge of the drum with the right index finger. A similar technique is used with the elbow in conga drumming. This technique produces an ascending pitch or descending pitch, if done in reverse, and can be executed on either the *hembra* or *macho.*

PITCH TECHNIQUE

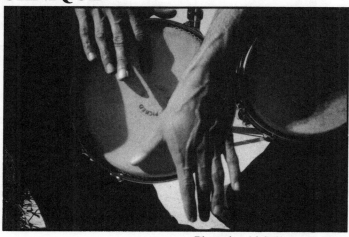

Photo by Al Salloum © 1995

One technique described by Humberto Morales in his text, *Latin-American Rhythm Instruction,* involves playing the bongo bell pattern on the shells of the bongos. The bongos are held upright on the knee, while striking the shells with a stick: the small shell plays the closed tone of the bell, while the *hembra* shell simulates the open tone of the cow bell. Although this technique is rarely used, it demonstrates the variety of application and the unlimited potential for creating sounds on the bongos.

BELL PATTERN ON BONGOS

Photo by Al Salloum © 1995

Instead of striking the bongos with the hands, occasionally, sticks are used. This technique can be employed for greater volume, especially when a more non-traditional approach is desired, i.e. in a rock setting or when the bongos are on stands. Sticks can also be used in simulating other percussion patterns where a stick is commonly utilized (e.g. *merengue, pa' cá).*

In Cuba many *bongoseros* will play a *maraca* and/or cowbell with their right hand while playing the bongos with their left. This is especially useful when extra percussionists are not available. The *bongosero* will often place the cowbell on a chair with a towel that limits movement and dampens the sound. Sometimes the cowbell is hit with a beater or a *maraca.*

MARACA/BELL TECHNIQUE

Photo by Al Salloum © 1995

maintenance

As mentioned previously, the bongo requires very little care and maintenance. As with any wooden instrument, try to avoid exposing bongos to rapid change in temperature. When moving from a cold to a heated environment allow time for the drums to adjust to the temperature change before playing. Rapid contraction and expansion of the wood may cause cracking between the wood staves. Occasional application of lug lubricant can prevent rust and facilitate easier adjusting of tension screws. Heads can be kept clean with a moist cloth.

The heads should always be loosened with a wrench when one is finished playing. This will preserve the life of the heads and prevent over stretching. The *macho* heads will require replacement more often than most hand drums because of their extremely high tension. The head can be replaced easily or a mounted head can usually be purchased from a music store.

HEAD REPLACEMENT

To change bongo heads you will need a few tools: long nose pliers, sharp knife, scissors, replacement skin with diameter of at least 4" greater than the shell, and skin wire about $1/16$" larger than the outside diameter of the crown.

BONGOS

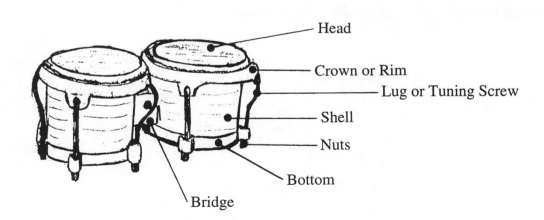

1) Separate *macho* and *hembra* at the bridge to permit easier rotation of the shell during head replacement.

2) Soak the new skin in lukewarm water until pliable; usually this will take about 1-2 hours for a thin head ($1/32$"-$1/16$")

3) Place skin over top of the shell. Determine the top side of the skin by lightly scraping your fingernail on skin. If it leaves a mark, this is the bottom of the skin. The top is more shiny and resistant to marking.

4) The next procedure is perhaps the most challenging. First place the skin wire on top of the skin, then gather the skin edges towards the center, placing the crown on top.

5) Attach the lugs to the nuts very loosely to allow movement of the skin.

6) Carefully pull the skin with pliers around the skin wire and under the crown, to rest between crown and shell of drum. The edges need to be pulled taut and uniformly around the circumference to remove wrinkles. A curved appearance to the underside of the skin is normal.

7) Once all the skin is pulled through, the lugs can be tightened just enough to bring the top of the crown about 1" from top of the head or about 1/4" above the desired playing position. As the head dries it will contract slightly.

8) The next step is trimming the excess skin. *Caution* should be exercised to avoid cutting the new head while trimming. Use the top of the crown as a guide. I usually trim with scissors or knife in one hand and pliers holding the skin in the other hand. Placing a flat piece of stiff cardboard between the cutting tool and the skin will help protect against nicking the new head.

9) Once mounted, the head is left to dry. This usually takes 1-2 days but will depend on humidity, thickness of the skin, etc. Make sure it is completely dry before tightening. Tighten clockwise, *gradually,* making sure the crown is parallel to the top of the shell. Use the same number of turns per screw to allow even tension. It is safer to wait for a few days of playing before tightening the head fully. Remember to slacken off tension of the screws after playing. This preserves the life and quality of the head.

Some bongo accessories that are useful include salve, finger tape, case, 1/2" wrench and pouch, extra skins, lug lube, metronome, drum machine and recordings of great *bongoseros* (see RESOURCES p.59).

Calendula salve is one of the most natural and beneficial substances for the skin of the hands. It acts as a lubricant, prevents cracking and enhances healing. It is available at most health food stores or pharmacies.

Sometimes **tape** may be necessary when playing for long periods or when hands have become too dry. Standard 1 $^1/_2$ cm waterproof adhesive tape works well and is available at most pharmacies.

Bongo cases help protect the drums and facilitate carrying of drums and accessories. Special cases are available from the major drum companies or other suitable canvas cases are available from army surplus stores that can be adapted for use.

Most bongos use $^1/_2$" bolts with corresponding tension screws. For convenience a **leather pouch** can easily be constructed from a few pieces of leather and lace to hold a $^1/_2$" wrench. This can be tied to the bongos and allows easy access when playing or transporting.

LEATHER POUCH FOR WRENCH

Photo by T. Salloum © 1995

Try to have a couple of **extra skins** for the *macho* which breaks more frequently. Skins are available from most drum stores or leather shops.

A **metronome** is a valuable tool to develop steady time for any musician. Moreover, a **drum machine** can be programmed to play clave or other percussion pattern. Practicing with a drum machine can allow you to hear how the *martillo* or variation fits with the other percussion instruments.

interviews

Jack Costanzo, 1959, from the *Learn to Play Bongo* LP.

JACK COSTANZO
Interview
March 5 and 26, 1995

T.S.   Where were you born and when?

J.C.   You'll never get when, but where you're welcome to *(laughs)* - Chicago, Illinois (north side).

T.S.   Who were your parents?

J.C.   Martin Costanzo, Virginia Jean Sances.

T.S.   Why did you choose the bongos?

J.C.   I was a dancer before I was a bongo drummer. Marda, one of my wives, was my dancing partner; then she was a singer in my first band. Later she changed her name to Marda Saxon as a stage name. We used bongos in our act.

T.S.   You're Italian, right?

J.C.   Right, originally from Chicago. My family is from Sicily.

T.S.   Can you talk a little about some of your early influences regarding bongos?

J.C.   There were none around Chicago.

T.S.   There were no contemporaries?

J.C.   No, I was fortunate to be the first one to get some exposure when I was in Stan Kenton's band in '47. That's when we introduced bongos into jazz.

T.S.   So you grew up in Chicago.

J.C.   Well, I left Chicago very early. When I met my wife-to-be and we became a professional dance team and we toured all over the mid-west. So I left Chicago when I was 15 or 16 years old.

T.S.   Where did you go from there?

J.C.   After touring for a year or two we went to New York...

T.S.   What kinds of drums do you prefer?

J.C.   Eventually I became a very well-known musician and I endorsed a pair of bongos call "Costanzo bongos" with a company called Valje. That's all I use. I was in at the beginning of that company. Eventually I withdrew from that endorsement.

T.S.   Do you have a preference for any type of skins?

J.C.   A mule skin when I can get it. They call them kip gut.

T.S.   Do you have any idea when the first tunable bongos came on the scene?

J.C.   The first pair I ever saw I bought from someone in 1946, but I think I sold them, because I was still heating them in 1947 with Kenton and when I was with Nat King Cole in '49 and '50.

T.S.   When were you with Nat Cole?

J.C.   I was with Nat Cole for almost five years from the end of 1949.

T.S.   How did that work out, adapting the *martillo* with the swing style of jazz?

J.C.   The problem was that you played eighth notes without adjusting some of the feelings. You were playing eighth notes against a guy playing jazz, playing a dotted eighth and a sixteenth on the hi-hat and it was a terrible contrast, friction. When the bongos finally did become used a lot in jazz, drummers and bass players were going crazy over the Latin guys playing eighth notes.

T.S.   Did you have congas, too?

J.C.   With Nat Cole I played mostly conga drums. I played bongo with Nat on a lot of records like "Go Bongo." Eighty percent of the time I played conga drums with Nat. It was used more as a swing instrument because we didn't use a regular drummer.

Jack Costanzo with the
Nat "King" Cole trio in 1949.

T.S.   Can you recommend a specific album that would best exemplify your style with Nat?

J.C.   There is a title of an album that I'm on called *The Best of the Nat King Cole Trio* (Capital). On it is a song called "Bop Kick." It is a good example of my style at that time, but through the years I've changed completely. I've learned an awful lot. Now I play better Latin than I did.

T.S.   Can you give me an example of how your style has changed?

J.C.   The style of playing rhythm hasn't changed. My time is the same. The broken rhythm parts of Latin playing – I've been able to do more with that than I did. With Kenton and Nat Cole I couldn't do that as well. I did solos but they're not the same kind of solos I would do now.

T.S.   Were these good experiences – playing with Kenton and Cole?

J.C.   Fantastic! Before that I had just worked with Latin bands. The Lecuona Cuban Boys, Rene Touzet, Bobby Ramos. That was from the beginning of 1946.

T.S.   I understand you played with Frank Sinatra?

J.C.   I recorded with Sinatra and I was on his TV shows. I did a recording with Sinatra called "I'm gonna live till I die." You have probably heard of it. It was a single.

T.S.   Were there other people you played with?

J.C.   Sure, you'll recognize a lot of them. After Nat Cole I worked with Peggy Lee. Then I worked with a frantic entertainer whose name was Frances Faye.

T.S.   I heard an album of hers that you played on.

J.C.   Was that called *Caught in the Act.* That's the one you should hear. It's on Cresendo or GNP. It's the same owner. That's a record I was really pleased with.

T.S.   I understand that you worked with Armando Peraza or José Mangual.

J.C.   I played with them, but didn't work with them. Armando and I are very good friends. When I was with Kenton, we recorded a song called "Peanut Vendor" which became very big. We used part of Machito's rhythm section on this record. José Mangual was on cowbell, Machito played *maracas,* Carlos Vidal played conga drums, and I was laying down bongos. Armando and I have never played in the same group, but I remember having a fabulous jam session with just he and I in San Francisco when I was with Nat Cole. In fact I still remember – I had such a ball! He's a marvellous player! Armando, besides being a great conga drummer, is a great bongo player. You should talk to Armando and Manny Oquendo. He's a typical marvellous bongo player of the last decade or so. You should know that Mongo Santamaria plays great bongos. One of the best that was ever around died some years back and he worked with Paul Anka for eight to nine years. His name was Chino Pozo. Chino was a great bongo drummer. I remember when I was in Cuba there was a bongo player named Ramoncito. I went to Cuba in '51, '53, and '55.

T.S.   I heard you were initiated into the *Nañigo.*

J.C.   No, that's not true. I was at a cult get-together with *batás* being played and they put the cross on my forehead. I never became a member of *Nañigo.* I've played some of the Santo music. I've recorded things in 6/8 like *Lucumi* and *Nañigo* style. They all came from Africa.

T.S.   One article I read felt the bongos were derived from the *batá.* Do you think there is any correspondence between the *batá* and the bongo?

J.C.   I hadn't thought about it until I saw a library book which I don't remember, but it was an African culture book with a background in instruments and I saw a picture of very crude bongos. You look at those drums and say, "My God, I would love to hit them."

T.S.   Could I ask you a question about the "moose call" or glissando techniques used on the *hembra?* The slide technique used on the early *son* recordings.

J.C.   That came from Haiti, I believe. It's easy to do on their drums because they have pigskin which is rough and you get the traction. It's more common on congas than bongos. Where the surface is slippery it's difficult.

T.S.   Can I ask you about your recordings with Crescendo/GNP records?

J.C.   I put out two albums. One with each label. I put out one called *Mr. Bongo.* That was 1956. It's a pretty good album, too. I'm quite sure it's GNP. The other one was *Viva Tirado* (1971) and that's on Crescendo. "Viva Tirado" is a song that was made popular by a group called "El Chicano."

T.S.   There is one called *Bongo Fever,* also.

J.C.   That's mine on Liberty label. I did about six albums for Liberty. I was in a contract with that company. *Bongo Fever* was done live at the famous "Garden of Allah" in Los Angeles, a club popular even in the days of Rudolph Valentino. They had little bungalows in the back. In the front there was a hang-out for movie stars, hookers, and the general public. There was a long bar and a seating area and down some steps to a round dance floor. That's where we worked. They rejuvenated it and instituted music again. That was around 1958-59. That was one of my most famous engagements in L.A. I loved it!

T.S.   What about a recording you did called *Dancing on the Sunset Strip?*

J.C.   Goodness, what album is that? Is that with Tony Martinez?

T.S.   I don't know, a friend just told me that you played on this album.

J.C.   They've been putting out compilations albums. There have been three or four with songs of mine on them. If people don't tell me about them I don't know they're out. I don't remember any album called *Dancing on the Sunset Strip,* that I have in my memory now. There are several albums of mine that the company went out of business and masters were sold to other companies. Have you ever heard of Tops?

I made the original with them called *Mr. Bongo Cha-Cha-Chá*. Since then three other companies have released it through the years – one on Clarion.

In 1994 some guy in Spain came out with that album on CD. That album has been released three or four times with different companies. That may be the reason for that title, *Dancing on the Sunset Strip*. None of my original records were named that. *[ed. note - we later discovered it was an album with Tony Martinez on GNP as Jack had originally thought]*

T.S.   How old were you when you started playing bongos, Jack?

J.C.   Six!

T.S.   Six years old?

J.C.   No, I'm kidding *[laughs]*. I was a dancer and was going to a ballroom in Chicago called "Mary Garden Ballroom"...around 1938. It had two ballrooms, one was an annex. The regular ballroom was where everyone danced straight dancing. The annex is where all the people who wanted to do Yolanda and Velez style danced. They allowed you to dance any way you wanted to, open dancing, high lifts and the whole bit. The owner of the dance hall, Mr. Rice, imported a Puerto Rican band to play in the annex for about two weeks and that was the first time any of us ever heard Latin music in the flesh. It was a band called Mario Dumont. In that band was a guy playing drums called Sapito; it means "little frog." He was a hunch back. On one of the numbers he came out on the floor and played bongos. My eyes went out of my head. I was about 13 - 14 years old.

T.S.   I would like to ask you about your future projects.

J.C.   I recorded two records of mainstream dance things that I'm very enthused about. I think they're very good and have a chart potential. One is called *Conguero* which is an original that I wrote. The other is a record that was originally recorded by Joe Cuba. Joe Cuba's *Push. Push. Push.* I made a modern arrangement of it. It's kind of a cooking record. Now I'm trying to get a company to take it over and release it.

T.S.   How would you summarize the role of the *bongosero* in the group? First in the Afro-Cuban group, then in jazz.

J.C.   The bongos have always been the salt and pepper of the rhythm section, as far as I was concerned. They added the spice and the little accents and things. We're talking Latin music now. In the old days (40's) bongos were played much differently than they are played now (in Latin bands). In those days there were less offbeat rhythms. In the old days they hinged more on the *martillo* throughout, then accents with the *martillo* itself and always back to the *martillo*. Today that's changed. You don't hear very much *martillo* and the sound is even flatter. In the old days the bongos had more of a melodic sound. There was a tonal quality to it. Now they are getting a real flat sound that I don't like as well...

T.S.   What about with jazz?

J.C.   With jazz you've got to be more cautious. You can't be as adventuresome. ... you can't get away with too many offbeats in an established jazz rhythm. If you build a wall between what you're doing and what the drummer and bass player is doing then you're not helping, you're not enhancing the rhythm at all...if you are playing the *martillo* which you're doing mostly in jazz (I can't visualize anything else). Unless you're doing a free form thing which I've done. If you're going to play straight be-bop jazz or straight time, there is very little room or reason to do many offbeats. Otherwise, you're going to get in the way of the drummer who's going to be hitting different things with the bass drum. He's going to be the main person in jazz, not the bongos. I have always made the point when playing straight jazz to play very little offbeat things. Sure an accent here and there – otherwise there's no point in your being there. You'd be surprised how [by] playing the straight *martillo* in jazz you can cook a rhythm section. Unless you realize when you're playing that you're adjusting what are eighth notes into a feeling of jazz, people don't know it; they think you're still playing eighth notes, because they're hearing eight beats. There is a feeling that's going on that you know you're doing to jazz. Other than the straight dicky .. dicky.. dicky..

docky.. so you can fit into what's happening. That's a feeling. If you don't get that, you're hurting the rhythm section. ...This must be my literary year *[laughs]*. A book came out with Marlon Brando that I'm in, in a few spots. I used to play a lot with Marlon many years ago. We used to jam quite a bit.

T.S.   What does he play?

J.C.   Marlon is a conga player, he loves congas. He was addicted to them in those days. We used to take them on the set and play in the dressing room between takes on *Guys and Dolls*. I did some of the sound takes. ...He wouldn't go anywhere without his drums. He used to call me from Europe. "Send me some skins." He was a fanatic! Also, he played well for a non- professional.

ARMANDO PERAZA
Interview
March 11, 1995

Armando Peraza, 1995
Photo by John Walker

T.S.   When were you born?

A.P.   I was born May 31,1924 in Havana, Cuba, man. (One city called Lawton Batista, a suburb of Havana)

T.S.   Who were your parents?

A.P.   My father was an architect; he built that city called Lawton. His name was José Peraza and my mother was Francisca.

T.S.   Do you have any children?

A.P.   Yes, I have one daughter.

T.S.   Is it true that you are a cousin to Mongo Santamaria?

A.P.   No, no, no, Mongo is a friend. When I started my career, Mongo, he had already been playing. Mongo was one of my favorites. I was a dancer and I used to go to all these places called the academy, watching Mongo play. I never expected to be a bongo player; my thing was athletics. I was a runner and I was a good baseball player. I would hang around and they would ask me to play. One was Conjunto Los Dandies (Chino Pozo's Conjunto) where Mongo was the bongo player. Conjunto Kubavana was where I really established myself around 1944-47. I used to go and play for the cabarets.

T.S.   When did you come to the U.S.?

A.P.   I came to the U.S. in 1949. I went to see Mongo in Mexico, because he was sick. Then we joined a group called The Cuban Diamond and we went to New York. We played in a place called the Latin Theatre. It was located at Madison Avenue and 125th Street at that time. We did a television show with Milton Berle at the Waldorf-Astoria. Then we played at one club called Havana Madrid. The owner was the manager: a boxer named Kid Gavilan. He was the champion of the world. When I arrived in New York I went to the Palladium with Machito's band. That night... Machito let me sit in and play. Charlie Parker was there. That was 1949. Machito had a record date. The drummer was Buddy Rich with Charlie Parker and Flip Phillips. The arranger was Chico O'Farrill. We recorded that album which was very successful. It was eventually a Latin/Jazz album. The name of the album, I forget it. *[ed. note - probably "Afro-Cuban Jazz Suite"]* I don't know if my name is there. As a matter of fact in that session there was José Mangual, too. I think also there was Louis Miranda. I played bongos and congas. In that year, 1947, I played with Dizzy Gillespie at the Blue Note in Chicago. I sat in with Dizzy, but I decided to go with Slim Gaillard not with Dizzy. That was 1949 or 1950.

T.S.   Where did you go from there?

A.P.   We played at the Appollo Theatre. I had the privilege to travel with Slim Gaillard all over the United States. This is when I arrived in California.

T.S.	Why did you choose California versus New York?
A.P.	I liked San Francisco you know. I played with quite a few people. As a matter of fact I played in the beginning with Dave Brubeck and Cal Tjader. I was the one who introduced Cal Tjader to playing Latin jazz.
T.S.	What year did you play with Cal Tjader, Armando?
A.P.	I think it was in the 60's. I made one album called *Ritmo Caliente.* Then I played with Cal Tjader quite a few years, close to eight or nine years. I made an album with Cal Tjader then, but I wasn't playing with Cal then. George Shearing arrived from New York and his bass player was Al McKibbon. Al McKibbon played with Dizzy Gillespie. When George Shearing arrived in California Al McKibbon told him there's a guy called Armando Peraza, because Candido made a few records with George Shearing. McKibbon told him there's a guy in California. He can play. I stayed with George Shearing twelve years. Then when I came back to California I started with Cal Tjader.
T.S.	What years did you play with Shearing?
A.P.	In the 50's man.
T.S.	60's also?
A.P.	Yes. Then I put in quite a few years with Santana. I started with Santana, I think it was the 70's.
T.S.	Did you play at Woodstock?
A.P.	No, no, I didn't play at Woodstock.
T.S.	On some of the albums?
A.P.	On a lot of albums. *Caravanserai* and *Boboleta,* all very successful albums. For me and Tom Coster the keyboard player, we brought a different evolution to the band. I put in quite a few years with Carlos. Then I retired in 1992.
T.S.	Can I ask, going back to when you were young, what attracted you to the bongos?
A.P.	...I used to like it but deeply I never wanted to be a musician, for the reason all the musicians who work after hours, they all get very sick. But I had a natural ability. Nobody taught me anything. I learned on my own from listening to records you know, in Cuba, in that environment.
T.S.	Who did you listen to? Sexteto Habanero?
A.P.	Oh, of course! All those guys and Mongo, you know. Oh, there was a lot of people. One guy called Feliberto and Yeyito.
T.S.	Do you know Andrés Sotolongo?
A.P.	I didn't know him well, but I heard of him. There was Antoli... God! It's too many people to remember now.
T.S.	Yes, it's a long time ago.
A.P.	40-50 years.
T.S.	So you learned on your own, no teacher?
A.P.	No teacher. I created my own technique. A lot of people right now play two or three congas. I used to do that... I used to play three congas and bongos at the same time. Find the album called *George Shearing on Stage* you can see that, on Capital records. I wrote a lot of songs with George Shearing.
T.S.	Can you give me some names of some recordings with your style?
A.P.	...mostly Cal Tjader and George Shearing. You have to find George Shearing *Latin Affair, Latin Escapade, Mood Latin.* That way you see my contribution to George Shearing's music. These are in the 50's and 60's. Then Cal Tjader *Ritmo Caliente.* There are quite a few albums I don't remember now.

T.S.	Did they ever make any films you might have been in?
A.P.	One with Cal Tjader, that's all. I don't remember the name.

T.S.	Who are your favorite *bongoseros?*
A.P.	It's hard to say, man, because there are too many good ones. There was one guy called Chino he used to play with Perez Prado. Yeyito was fantastic! Chino Pozo was fantastic! Too many, it's hard to say. We had one guy in Cuba he never had the recognition. He was a master. His name was Mario. He used to play with a Conjunto called "Bolero." In that environment I was surviving. I have recognition in Cuba for my contribution on bongos. Then Patato Valdez played with me. He played congas with me in the Conjunto Kubavana. Patato Valdez was one of the creators. Very melodic. He played with Machito. A lot of people learned a lot of things from Patato. Don't let anybody fool you.

T.S.	Did anyone do a story on you?
A.P.	I was selected by the Smithsonian Institute for the Center for Jazz History because of all the different jazz musicians I played with.

T.S.	What about the slide technique, the glissando that sounds like a growl? When they slide the finger across the *hembra?*
A.P.	It's hard to describe it because everybody has a different technique. I used to use fingers, slap and combinations, giving a different characteristic to the bongos. What happens is, for different movements musically, you have to have a disciplinary approach to play. *Bolero* is played differently. *Son montuno* is played differently, *guaracha* is played differently. Each has a different conception...
	Today bongos have a lot of freedom. Today the music we play, especially jazz, has a lot of different influences. European influence, Brazil influence, Afro-Cuban influence. It is no longer jazz that you used to see with Count Basie, Benny Goodman. You understand what I mean? Jazz today is different.

T.S.	How do you feel the role of the *bongosero* has changed from the 30's or 40's to now?
A.P.	Not too much because I see all these people play a lot of things I used to play .... you put me with the music, I play with the music. I move my musicality according to the music that I am interpreting. If it's Cuban music, I play the Cuban style. If it is American music I try to fit myself to the American music. Too many people stay traditional. I can play traditional, but mostly what I try to do is move according to the music I am playing.

T.S.	I understand you wrote some songs?
A.P.	Oh, a lot of songs, man. Mongo recorded for me, Santana... I made a lot of music with Santana.

T.S.	What kind of drums do you like to use and what skins?
A.P.	...the natural skin is the real thing, but I want to explain to you something. A lot of people say to you this conga is no good, this bongo is no good. The problem is you control the bongos, the bongos don't control you. I can play on a piece of wood, right... People expect the bongo will play for them. You have to play the instrument. I don't care what it is. I have to make a sound. I find a way to make a sound.

T.S.	When did you have your first tunable bongo?
A.P.	Oh, a long time ago. I was one of the first to have that.

T.S.	What year did you have a tunable bongo?
A.P.	Probably around 1945. It was made for this guy, he was a drummer: Serevino - in Havana, you know. I brought it here to the United States.

T.S.	So when you came to the U.S., you were not heating up your drum heads.
A.P.	No, not here; in Cuba, yes. I used to use a special lamp that we created with kerosene and then we tuned it. We used to use a skin called *"pengamino."* Came from like a very young cow. All the bongos in

Cuba were mahogany and they still are. There was a guy in my country that Mongo used, right there in my neighborhood called Velgada. He made all these Cuban congas and bongos. One solid piece and I still have it! ...

T.S.   Armando, I don't want to take up a lot of your time.

A.P.   No, no, it's a pleasure, man. It's a pleasure...

T.S.   Thank you. Thank you very much!

JOSÉ MANGUAL
Interview
March 19, 1995

T.S.   Who were your earliest influences?

J.M.   Isaac Olviedo was a *tres* player in Cuba. When I was a kid about nine years old I heard a record that was playing in the street. I was listening to this fabulous *tres* player. That opened the door for me to play Cuban music...

T.S.   Do you know who the bongo player was?

J.M.   I don't know because we didn't have too much of the Cuban players coming to Puerto Rico to play. They would come in sporadically. I used to hear a program from San Juan every day from 12-1. Septeto Puerto Rico was the name of the group and they had a bongo player. That's how I became interested in playing the bongos.

José Mangual
Photo by Martin Cohen

T.S.   Can I ask you about the equipment you use? Do you have any preferences for the drums or skins?

J.M.   I like the wooden bongos and the skins have to be high pitched, not too thick (medium). On the island we used goat, but here we use calf.

T.S.   Do you like mahogany or oak bongos?

J.M.   Oak is the best one. It's a little heavier but lasts a long time and better sound.

T.S.   You played with Arsenio Rodriguez I understand?

J.M.   I recorded with him - just recorded with him.

T.S.   And Machito?

J.M.   That was really the first professional band I worked with here in this country (U.S.). Starting in 1942, the spring of 1942.

T.S.   When did you first start using the tunable bongo?

J.M.   I started doing that, since I first began playing. On the island they didn't use sterno because the climate over there is very damp. The drums, you couldn't get them to a high pitch with sterno.

T.S.   What year did you start playing?

J.M.   I started playing professionally in 1939.

T.S.   And you were using the tunable bongos?

J.M.   Yes! I'm pretty sure, it's because of the climate. You know the damper it is, the lower they get and you have trouble tuning them. The easiest way was to have tunables.

T.S.   How long did you stay with Machito?

J.M.   Sixteen years (1942-59)... then I left Machito to go with Herbie Mann for about 6-7 months. Then I freelanced and did some recordings in the city, and jingles. Then I went to the country to the Concord Hotel. It's a big hotel, very well known. I worked with an Italian fellow - Sonny Rossi. I worked with him for about three years. Then I left and worked freelance with some singers. One who used to sing with Cugat. I can't remember her name.

T.S.   You also worked with Erroll Garner?

J.M.   I worked with him from 1967 'til he died in 1977.

T.S.   Did you play bongos with him as well as congas?

J.M.   I used to play both. On a trip to Canada I forgot them in the cab *[laughs]* and I played congas. It was better because you can groove more and add more body to it. The bongos are a little too thin. With the bongos you always need a conga player next to you.

T.S.   You played with Dizzy [Gillespie]?

J.M.   I played concerts with Dizzy. We played quite a few Carnegie concerts.

T.S.   Basie also? [Count Basie]

J.M.   I recorded with Basie, I didn't play with Basie.

T.S.   Cal Tjader?

J.M.   I made a recording with Cal Tjader playing *timbales [laughs]*. I never heard it, but I didn't think it turned out too good.

T.S.   Can you name some records that provide an example of your style? I have one called *Buyu* put out by LP, but perhaps you can name others?

J.M.   For Dizzy I made one of the "Manteca" versions, that made a good solo. There is one with a good solo on Charlie Parker's album called *South of the Border* and there are quite a few with Willie Bobo's group (the Latin jazz group). I played on all those recordings on bongos.

T.S.   Do you use much ornamentation in your playing like "the moose call," etc?

J.M.   No, I've got my style. It's an awkward style *[laughs]*... when I was young we didn't have a lot of people playing... now you have a million players. You can listen to this one, then to another and more or less create your own style.

T.S.   How would you define the role of the *bongosero* playing jazz versus Latin?

J.M.   The thing that really fits in there is the conga drum. The bongo doesn't fit unless you have a conga drummer next to you. You could do it, but it doesn't sound as good. You can play things like *Masacote*. I made some concerts with Lionel Hampton, Patato and I. Then we could do something that sounded a little better, you know. In jazz the *martillo* doesn't fit that well. You have to improvise. You play a lot of solos/fills.

T.S.   Are you working on any projects now?

J.M.   My sons and I are going to make an album. I'm writing some music. I never wrote much in the past.

T.S.   You've lived in New York many years?

J.M.   I've lived in New York since I migrated to this country. I came in 1939. I always lived over here in Harlem. It was a different life. It's been very good to me. I have no regrets. People always say, "Oh, you live in Harlem with all those people." Nothing ever happens here. I think it happens to all the guys doing the wrong things. That happens everywhere.

T.S.   I understand you're good friends with Armando Peraza. Did you ever play with Armando Peraza?

J.M. Peraza, I played with him since he first came over here to this country. We played a show over here in east Harlem (Spanish Harlem). We played at a theatre called "The Hispanic Theatre" (Theatro Hispano). I played also at Havana Madrid Club in 1942 with Machito. We used to play Sunday matinee. It was 51st and Broadway. It was a basement.

T.S. I understand you've played more bongos than congas.

J.M. I never played congas until I came to this country, because if you know the black history against the white history. All those privileges were taken away from us. There were places that were too big and too many slaves that they let them play drums. They would revolt you know. But the small little islands that they could control a little better they didn't let you play. The first conga drum that I saw was when I came over here. I was 14 years old. Then after that I never played the conga drum, just bongos.

T.S. Who are some of your favorite *bongoseros?*

J.M. My favorite *bongosero* is Peraza. I think he's the greatest bongo player I've heard.

CANDIDO CAMERO
Interview
March 29, 1995

T.S. Why did you start to play the bongos and conga drums?

C.C. It was inspiration from my uncle on my mother's side, when I was four years old.

T.S. I understand you were from Havana.

C.C. Yes, Havana, Cuba. I was born in El Cerro district.

T.S. Was that in the 30's or 20's?

C.C. That was the late 20's.

T.S. At that time they didn't have tunable bongos, did they?

C.C. We used to tune it with...ah

T.S. Sterno?

Candido Camero
Photo by Martin Cohen

C.C. No, not even sterno. Sterno was over here in the United States. When I came over here in 1946, that's when I started using sterno. ... sometimes we used newspaper with matches, and we light the newspaper and we use the flame. Most of the time we burn the skins because it was too hot.

T.S. Who was your first influence?

C.C. My uncle... his name was Andrés Guerra. That was my grandfather's last name.

T.S. Did you used to listen to a lot of groups when you were a little boy?

C.C. Yes, he used to take me every time they would have rehearsals. He used to take me with him all over, everywhere they have rehearsals.

T.S. Were you familiar with groups like Septeto Habanero?

C.C. Oh, yeah. Sexteto Habanero, Septeto Nacional and Boloña. These were the pioneers.

T.S. Do you know about the *chanqüi* style?

C.C. No, that might be a different era.

T.S.   Can you tell me what kind of bongo you like to use?

C.C.   Right now I'm using the Latin Percussion.

T.S.   Do you like the oak?

C.C.   Yes, I have the big ones....must be the "original" model because they're big.

T.S.   What kind of skin?

C.C.   The ones that come with the bongos.

T.S.   What are some good recordings of your style on the bongos?

C.C.   I have so many.

T.S.   Which would be the best?

C.C.   Every one has a bongo solo or conga solo, every one of my records....They are all good. I never recommend one because they are all good.

T.S.   Which records do you have on your own?

C.C.   On my own I have about 50. The people I record with, the people on my list I have recorded with, I have 100 different names.

T.S.   Were you in any movies or films?

C.C.   Oh yes, a couple of them.

T.S.   Do you remember any names?

C.C.   Well, I did a couple in Cuba with Sonora Mantancera (later 40's or 50's). Also, I did movies at the Tropicana night club where I used to work in Cuba with the famous Argentinian singer Liberty Demarco. I did other movies, too.

T.S.   I would like to ask you the names of your CDs with the most drumming?

C.C.   The ones on my own, every one of them. There are two that came out now on CD. One called *Brujerias de Candido* (Tico).

T.S.   What does that mean?

C.C.   It's just a name. In Spanish it's like "African voodoo." The album has nothing to do with voodoo. That's the producer's idea. He's the one that gives the name *[laughs]*. The other one that came out recently is *Candido Beautiful* (Blue Note). A lot of bongos and congas there. *Candido Beautiful* just came out on CD.

T.S.   I want to ask you about the musicians. I know you played with Dizzy Gillespie.

C.C.   Wait 'til you see the list[1] I'm going to send you. The list on the jazz field and the list on the Latin field.

T.S.   When you play jazz on bongos, what is your approach?

C.C.   It's a different style altogether between Latin and jazz. Different feeling. You have to play with the feel of the music. I approach it by listening to what's going on with the music... the arrangement and the type of rhythm.

---

[1] Candido's bio is extensive, listing numerous performances including "Birdland" with Dizzy Gillespie, Charlie Parker and Miles Davis. He is pictured in *The World Book Encyclopedia* (1960) in the listing under Drums and is featured in Herman Leonard's book *The Eye of Jazz* (Viking Press). Candido has over 100 recording credits: Duke Ellington, Woody Herman, Art Blakey, Wes Montgomery, Kenny Clarke, Ray Charles, George Shearing, Kenny Burrell, Tony Bennet, Erroll Garner, Dinah Washington, Sonny Rollins, Stan Getz, Elvin Jones, Buddy Rich, Charles Mingus, and Mongo Santamaria.

T.S. Do you think the style of playing has changed in the last 30 to 40 years?

C.C. No.

T.S. Still lots of *martillo?*

C.C. Oh, yes. That's the foundation of the whole thing.

T.S. Did you ever play with bongos and congas all together at one time?

C.C. At the same time I play bongos and congas....conga and *quinto*....three congas, cowbell, *güiro*. All together at the same time by myself. The three congas, the cowbell and the *güiro* at the same time, while singing too. Sometime I play the bongo and the conga at the same time. Some time I play the bongo and the *quinto* at the same time.

T.S. Who are some of your favorite *bongoseros?*

C.C. They are all good. Everyone has their own style. That's what makes the music so interesting.

T.S. Do you still practice?

C.C. No, no, because I'm so busy recording, playing concerts. I'm travelling all the time.

T.S. Do you have some new projects coming up?

C.C. Well, I'm working now on a recording. Another solo album.

6/8 - Common time signature in Afro-Cuban music, indicating six eighth notes to the bar.

BATA - Double headed drums of an hour glass shape derived from music of the *Yorubas* of Nigeria. Usually in sets of three, used in both secular and sacred music.

BEMBE - African derived rhythm, predominantly 6/8, played at special gatherings. Also refers to drums used at these special ceremonies.

BOLERO - Slow Afro-Cuban rhythm and dance similar to a ballad.

BOMBA - Puerto Rican rhythm and dance usually containing lyrics on social struggle.

BONGOSERO - Player of the bongo drums.

BOSSA NOVA - A rhythm integrating jazz and Brazilian influences; popularized in the 1950's.

BOTIJA -A clay oil jug used as a wind instrument to provide the bass in early *son*.

CALENDULA SALVE - A herbal agent used historically for promoting healing of the skin.

CAMPANA - Cowbell

CASCARA - Pattern played on sides of the *timbales*/congas/*gua gua* also referred to as *paila* or *palito* pattern.

CENCERRO - cowbell

CHA CHA CHA - Dance derived from the *mambo,* but slower, sweeter and less syncopated. First written evidence by Enrique Jorrin, 1951.

CHANGUI - Rural style of eastern Cuban music that developed in the late 1800's.

CLAVE - Rhythm that forms the basis of most Afro-Cuban music. A five-note pattern. Usually conceived in North America as a two-bar phrase with three beats in the first and two in the second.

CLAVES - Two pieces of resonant wood that play the clave pattern.

CONGA - (drum) Afro-Cuban single headed, barrel shaped drum, three main sizes, smallest to largest: *quinto,* conga, *tumbadora.*

CONGA - (rhythm) Carnival rhythm and dance with both Santiago and Havana styles.

CONJUNTO - An ensemble of specific instruments combining vocal, guitars, *maracas,* clave, trumpets and later adding congas, bongos and piano.

CROWN - Metal circular collar that sits on top of the drum and holds the drum head in position.

DANZON - Ballroom style dance that developed in the late 1800's, containing European influences.

DISTAL - A position farthest from the center of the body, the opposite of proximal.

ENTERIZO - Drums constructed from one piece of wood as opposed to wood staves glued together.

FLAM - A flam consists of playing a grace note with the opposite hand just slightly before the main note. Both notes have the same count.

GLISSANDO - A slide or growl technique performed on the drum head for special effects (AKA - moose call).

GUA GUA - Instrument constructed from a piece of bamboo placed on a stand and struck with two sticks. The *cáscara* pattern is played on the *gua gua* when playing the *rumba.*

GUAGUANCÓ - A medium tempo *rumba,* played on three conga drums with other percussion and vocals. An Afro-Cuban rhythm and couple dance.

GUAJIRA - A slow rural style music with Spanish influence originally played on the *tres* (guitar) with vocals and percussion.

GUARACHA - A quick rhythm and dance of rural Cuban origin, originally having satirical lyrics.

HEMBRA ("female" in Spanish) - The largest of the two bongo drums.

INDEX FINGER - First finger after the thumb.

LUG - Metal tuning rod (screw) of the bongo/conga drums.

MACHO ("male" in Spanish) - Smallest of the two bongo drums.

MAMBO ("chant" in Congolese) - Dance influenced by Congolese religious cults. Developed in the 1940's and popularized by Perez Prado, Arsenio Rodriquez and Arcano y sus Maravillas.

MANOTEO - Alternating heel and toe pattern played on the bongos during the *martillo* and other rhythms, usually with the left hand.

MARACAS - Rattles originally made from gourds or leather, filled with seed, beans, or pebbles.

MARIMBULA - Large adaptation of African thumb piano used to provide the bass in early *son* and *rumba.*

MARTILLO ("hammer" in Spanish) - The basic rhythm of the bongos upon which all improvisation is based

MASACOTE - African rhythm, medium to fast, in 4/4, involving improvised exchange between drummers.

MERENGUE - Dance and rhythm of the Dominican Republic. A fast 2/4, usually played with a metal *güiro* and *tambora* (double head drum).

MONTUNO - The section of the musical piece where the call and response occurs and solos are played. In the *montuno* the *bongosero* usually plays cowbells.

MOOSE CALL - Same as glissando.

OFFBEATS - Upbeats or beats that occur midway between the downbeats in a bar.

PA CA - Creole rhythm believed to be developed by Juanito Marquez.

PLENA - Puerto Rican rhythm in 2/4, usually played with *panderetas* (tambourine without jingles).

PROXIMAL - A position closest to the body center, versus distal.

QUINTO - Smallest of the three conga drums. Usually the solo drum in *rumba.*

RHUMBA - Popular music/dance of the U.S. in the 50's. Actually adaptation of the *son.* Not to be confused with *rumba.*

RUMBA - Popular music/dance of Cuba. Three basic styles; *guaguancó, columbia, yambu* which incorporates vocals, drums and percussion.

RUMBEROS - Players of *rumba.*

SALSA ("sauce" in Spanish) - Modern day *son* of North America, developed in the 1960's -1970's.

SAMBA - Brazilian rhythm/dance - upbeat tempo 2/4.

SEPTETO - Seven piece *son* group, developed subsequent to the *sextetos* around 1920's - *tres,* guitar, bongos, clave, bass, *maracas*/vocals, trumpet.

SEXTETO - Six piece similar to *septeto* without trumpet.

SON - Probably the oldest and most popular musical style of Cuba, developed around the late 1800's in Oriente province.

SON MONTUNO - Derivation of the *son* musical style with a clear improvised section *(montuno).*

SONGO - A contemporary rhythm containing elements of various Cuban and North American styles. *Songo* became popularized by groups such as Los Van Van of Cuba.

STERNO - A can containing fuel used to heat drum heads for tuning, before metal tuning rods were developed.

THENAR EMINENCE - Fleshy part of tissue at the base of the thumb (palm side).

TRES - A Cuban-styled guitar with three double strings. Essentially an instrument of the early *son* made popular by Arsenio Rodriguez.

TUMBAO - Repeated rhythmical pattern for the conga drums. It provides the foundation for the instrument similar in function to the *martillo* with the bongos.

UPBEATS - Same as offbeats.

resources

The most important resource for the bongo student is a collection of recordings of the great *bongoseros*. Many of these recordings are now readily available. Some of the early recordings have been re-issued on Latin and world music labels. The following, although not complete, lists some notable *bongoseros* and groups with whom they have performed.

• Augustín Gutiérrez (Sexteto Habanero, Trio Matamoros, Bene More)

• José Manual Incharte "El Chino" (Sexteto Habanero, Sexteto Boloña, Septeto Nacional)

• Andres Sotolongo (Sexteto Habanero, Isacc Olviedo)

• Rogelio Castellano (Septeto Nacional de Ignacio Pinero)

• Miguel Angel Portillo (Septeto Nacional).

• Antolín Suarez "Papa Kila" (Arsenio Rodriguez)

• Chino Pozo (Perez Prado, Fats Navarro, Paul Anka, Tito Puente, Eddie Palmieri)

• Chano Pozo (Dizzy Gillespie)

* José Mangual Sr. (Arsenio Rodriguez, Cal Tjader, Erroll Garner, Tito Puente, Machito, Herbie Mann, Count Basie, Dizzy Gillespie, Willie Bobo, Charlie Parker, Sarah Vaughan, Dexter Gordon, Stan Kenton, Stan Getz, Eddie Palmieri, Carmen MaCrae, Frank Morgan, Billy Taylor, Cachao)

• Armando Peraza (Conjunto Kubavana, Cal Tjader, George Shearing, Slim Gaillard, Santana, John McLaughlin, Wes Montgomery, Linda Ronstadt, Machito, Gato Barbieri, Aretha Franklin, John Lee Hooker, Eric Clapton, Alice Coltrane, Roy Buchanan)

* Mongo Santamaria (Perez Prado, Tito Puente, Dizzy Gillespie)

* Candido Camero (Dizzy Gillespie, Charles Mingus, Dexter Gordon, Stan Kenton, Billy Taylor, Coleman Hawkins, Woody Herman, George Shearing, Erroll Garner, Duke Ellington, Charlie Parker, Machito, Tito Puente)

• Bill Alvarez (Cozy Cole)

* Roberto Roena

• Sabu Martinez (Dizzy Gillespie)

• José "Papo" Rodriguez (Tito Puente, Poncho Sanchez)

- Jack Costanzo (Nat King Cole, Stan Kenton, Frank Sinatra, Peggy Lee, Francis Faye)
- Johnny "Dandy" Rodriguez (Tito Puente, Charlie Palmieri)
- Humberto "Nengue" Hernandez (Cachao, Mongo Santamaria)
- Anthony Carrillo (Batacumbele, Eddie Palmieri, Descarga Boricua)
- David Romero (Poncho Sanchez, Earth Wind & Fire)
- Louis Rivera (Rubén Blades)

* Manny Oquendo (Libre, Eddie Palmieri, Tito Puente, Chano Pozo, Tito Rodriguez, Johnny Pacheco, Larry Harlow)

- Willie Bobo (Mongo Santamaria, Tito Puente)
- Jose L. Quintana "Chanquito" (Los Van Van)
- Willie Rosario (Alegre Allstars)
- Luis Gonzalez (Ray Barretto)
- José Mangual Jr. (Mario Bauza, Rubén Blades, Willie Colon)
- Ray Romero (Eddie Palmieri, Tito Puente, Machito, Xavier Cugat, Tito Rodriguez)

* Giovanni Hidalgo (Eddie Palmieri, Tito Puente)

- Victor Gonzales (Ismael Rivera)
- William Rodriguez (Stan Kenton, Johnny Hartman, Cal Tjader)
- Luis Mangual (Johnny Pacheco, Celia Cruz)

* John Santos (Tito Puente, Pete Escovedo)

- Marc Quiñones (Celia Cruz, Allman Brothers)
- Louis Bauzó (Mongo Santamaria)
- Tommy "Choki" Lopez (Eddie Palmieri)
- Pablo Cortés Gonzales (NG La Banda)
- Luis Chacon (Paulito Y Su Elite)
- José Miguel Velazquez (Manolin el Medico de la Salsa)
- Clemente "Chicho" Piquero (Pérez Prado, Beny Moré)
- Rogelio "Yeyito" Iglesias (Israel "Cachao" Lopez)
- Javier Oquendo (Eddie Palmieri)
- Paoli Mejías (Eddie Palmieri, Deddie Romero)
- José Madera (Tito Puente)
- Nicky Marrero (Dizzy Gillespie, Ismael Rivera, Nueva Manteca, Eddie Palmieri)
- Mike Pacheco (Stan Kenton, Shorty Rogers, Nat King Cole, Perez Prado)

* appears as leader on some recordings

bibliography

Brown, Thomas A. *Afro-Latin Rhythm Dictionary.* Alfred Publishing Co. Inc., Sherman Oaks, CA., 1984.

Clarke, Donald (ed). *Penguin Encyclopedia of Popular Music.* Viking (Penguin Group), London, 1989.

Cruz, Tomás. Escuela Nacional de Arte de Cuba. Havana - lecture notes, 1994.

Descarga Catalog Version. 1.5 Brooklyn, N.Y., 1994/95.

Duran, Lucy. "In Pursuit of Son," *Folk Roots.* No. 67., Southern Rag LTD., London, England, Jan., 1989.

Gerard, Charley with Marty Sheller. *Salsa: The Rhythm of Latin Music.* White Cliffs Media Company, Crown Point, IN. 1989.

Joe Montego. "Bongos," *Modern Percussionist.* Vol. I No. 3, Modern Drummer Pub., Cedar Grove, N.J., June 1985.

Kinkle, Roger D. *The Complete Encyclopedia of Popular Music and Jazz 1900-1950.* Vol II, Arlington House Pub., N.Y., 1974.

Latin Percussion. *Understanding Latin Rhythms Vol II.* Latin Percussion Inc., Palisades N.J., 1977.

Llerenas, Eduardo. "The Cuban Son and Septet," *Septetos Cubanos.* Liner notes, Musica Tradicional, Colonia Hipodrono Condesa, Mexico. 1990.

Ludwig, Wm. F. *Modern Jazz Drumming.* Ludwig Drum Co., Chicago, IL., 1958.

Malabe, Frank and Bob Weiner. *Afro-Cuban Rhythms for Drumset.* Manhattan Music Inc., N.Y., N.Y., 1990.

Mauleon, Rebeca. *Salsa Guide book for Piano and Ensemble.* Sher Music Co., Petaluma, CA., 1993.

Morales, Humberto. *Latin American Rhythm Instruments.* Henry Alder Pub Co. N.Y., 1954.

Quintana, José Luis (Changuito) lecture notes. Afrocubanismo, Banff Centre for the Arts, Banff, 1994.

Reed, Ted. *Progressive Steps to Bongo and Conga Drum Technique.* Ted Reed Pub., Clearwater, FL., 1961.

Sanabria, Roberto. "Candido Legendary Congero," *Highlights in Percussion.* Vol. 3, No. 1, Latin Percussion. N.J. 1988.

Santos, John. *La Historia del Son Cubano the Roots of Salsa, Vol II* liner notes. Folkloric Records 9054 "Mounting Conga and Bongo Heads," *Modern Percussionist.* Vol. 1 No. 3, Modern Drummer Pub., Cedar Grove, N.J. June 1985.

Stone, George Lawrence. *Stick Control for the Snare Drummer.* George B Stone & Son Inc., Boston, MA., 1963.

Sulsbrück, Birger. *Latin - American Percussion Rhythms and Rhythm Instruments from Cuba* (Video). Wilhelm Hansen AS, Copenhagen. 1988.